The
Golden
Ball

The Golden Ball

The Fairy Tale of the Frog Prince and Why the Princess Kissed Him

Katelyn Sinclair

Chthonicity Press

RICHMOND, CALIFORNIA

Published by Chthonicity Press, Richmond, California, USA
Contact: books@chthonicity.com

First Edition

ISBN 978-1-937186-00-5 (Hardcover)

Library of Congress Control Number: 2011933682
Library of Congress subject headings:
      Fairy tales.
      Fairy tales--Adaptations.
      Children's stories.
      Children's poetry.
      American poetry.
      Princesses--Juvenile literature.
      Animals--Juvenile poetry.

Poem text typeset in Paracelsus Pro
Artwork created in Adobe Photoshop

Retold in rhymed iambic tetrameter from "The Frog Prince" by the Brothers Grimm

With special thanks to Eric and Jason for their invaluable suggestions

To hear Katelyn read this book aloud, please visit her on the web
at www.katelynsinclair.com

For my sister

An infant princess once was born
Upon an early winter morn
So long ago and far away
Her name is lost to us today.

But this we know: She was so fair
That all who saw her stopped to stare.
The Sun himself would pause and sigh
Each day he journeyed through the sky.

Now, this land was far north of here,
And frozen through most of the year,
So for the Sun to hover hence
Could not be a coincidence.

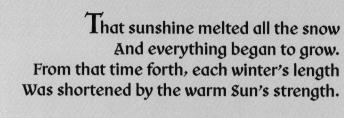

That sunshine melted all the snow
And everything began to grow.
From that time forth, each winter's length
Was shortened by the warm Sun's strength.

Abundant springs and summers came,
And with them grew the baby's fame.
Because he loved her most of all,
The Sun gave her a golden ball.

It's no surprise the princess grew
An ego large enough for two.
She thought herself above the rest—
A notion which life soon would test.

The princess didn't like to stay
Inside the castle walls all day.
She'd sneak outside and off she'd go,
Down to the forest far below.

Enchanted eyes watched as she played;
A prince was hiding in the shade.
A spell cast by an evil queen
Had made his skin turn rather green.

The prince had heard a prophecy
This royal maid could set him free.
He knew her by her golden ball,
The sign the Sun had come to call.

One day, she stole into the wood
A little further than she should.
She came upon a lovely pond
And sunny meadow just beyond.

The princess laughed with sheer delight.
The frog prince wished with all his might
A moment when he could contrive
To meet her would at last arrive.

The princess frolicked in the glade.
She chased her ball into the shade.
She ran in circles 'round the lake
And then she made a big mistake.

The princess threw her ball so high
She saw two suns up in the sky.
She ran to catch it as it fell,
But didn't do it very well.

For suddenly, the poor girl slipped,
And then she stumbled, and she tripped,
And then she fell, and with a thud
She landed in some puddled mud.

The ball plunged down, a golden flash
That landed with a giant splash.
She stretched out on the muddy bank
But couldn't reach it.

Then it sank.

Her situation was quite grim.
"Alas," she wept, "I cannot swim!"
And, soaking wet, she hung her head
And cried until her eyes turned red.

"It's now or never," thought the frog.
He hopped up on a floating log.
"Hello," he croaked. She simply stared.
He was so strange that she felt scared.

The frog said, "Princess, I confess
I noticed you were in distress.
I beg you, please don't cry or pout,
For we can help each other out."

"Oh, frog," she sobbed, "my ball is lost.
I'd have it back at any cost.
Although this might sound very bold,
I'd give up all my jewels and gold."

"I'd love to help," the sly frog said,
"But this is what I'd like instead:
If I retrieve your golden ball,
You'll take me to the castle hall,
And there we'll eat and sleep and play
Together each and every day."

The princess thought, "That can't be true!
Frogs cannot live like people do."

She doubted that he would succeed,
But just in case, the girl agreed.
"Dear frog," she said, "please do your best.
I pledge to honor your request."

The frog let out a whoop of joy.
He dove down deep to find her toy.
The princess paced; she understood
Her ball was likely lost for good.

The frog resurfaced with a gasp,
The gold ball tightly in his grasp.
"Oh, thank you, frog!" she cried with glee.
She eyed her plaything greedily.

She reached for it.
He hopped away.

He said,
"First, princess, let us play.
For now that we are friends, you see,
You ought to share your toys with me."

She did not like this frog at all.
She did not want to share her ball.
To get it back, she would pretend
The frog was now her dearest friend.

So once again the princess lied.
"Of course, let's play!" she gaily cried.

"All right, then catch!" the frog agreed,
And threw the ball with extra speed.

She jumped and caught it with a twist,
Rejoicing that she hadn't missed.

"Now throw it back!" her new friend said.
The princess laughed and shook her head.

She clutched the ball and turned around.
The frog feared she was homeward bound.
She tucked her wet skirts up with ease
And ran away into the trees.

She was too fast to intercept.
When she was gone, the poor frog wept.
She'd tricked him with her clever lies,
But he would plan a big surprise.

The princess sat to dine that night
With a voracious appetite.
Mid-bite she heard the strangest sound.
She dropped her fork and looked around.

'Twas followed by an angry knock,
And something shouted through the lock.
"O princess! Open up this door!
Do you remember what you swore?"

At once, her eyes grew very wide.
A twinge of panic flared inside.
She pushed away her golden plate
And ran off to investigate.

She opened up the castle door
And what she saw there scared her more.
The frog had found her, though she'd run!
She understood then what she'd done.

The frog said, "Sorry to be late.
If you recall, we have a date."
The princess slammed the door and fled
Back to the dining hall instead.

And there she sat and shook with fright.
Her face had turned a ghostly white.
The king asked, "Who calls here so late?
Is there a monster at the gate?"

"It is a frog," the princess said.
"To see him here fills me with dread."

Her father asked, "What does he seek?"

The princess found it hard to speak.

"That ball of which I am so fond
Was lost today, deep in a pond.
The frog retrieved my orb of gold
When I was wet and sad and cold.
I promised him
he'd live with me—
My friend until eternity.
I swear to you, now,
in my shame,
I didn't think
he'd make his claim."

The king knew he could not dismiss
A revelation such as this.
His daughter was a spoiled brat.
She must be stopped, and that was that.

He said, "Child, you cannot retract
A pledge, vow, promise, oath or pact,
So there is no point in denial.
Go greet your new friend with a smile."

She stamped her foot, and in her fear,
The princess screamed for all to hear,
"He is a frog! It makes no sense
To say I owe him recompense!"

"I've heard enough!"
her father roared.
"Young lady,
you cannot afford
To argue with me.
You won't win.
Now keep your word
and let him in."

The princess slunk with wounded pride
To fetch the frog who sat outside.
She stalked back with a sullen air
And flung him down upon a chair.

The king said, "Welcome, frog, at last.
Please help yourself to our repast.
My daughter says you're here to stay;
She has a big debt to repay."

The frog replied, "Your majesty,
I thank you for receiving me."
He bowed, and with a little hop
He jumped up on the tabletop.

For hours,
the king and frog conversed.
They ate their fill
and quenched their thirst.
The princess
couldn't eat a bite.
She worried
they might talk
all night.

But then, at last, the frog professed
That it was time for him to rest.
"Dear princess, let us go to bed.
In which room do you lay your head?"

"Oh, no," she said, "that will not do.
The dungeon is what's fit for you."

The king said, "Absolutely not!
My daughter, you were better taught!
The dungeon simply would not be
Sufficient hospitality."

The princess sighed.
She knew she'd lost.
She hoped her ball
was worth the cost.

Her bedroom had a giant bed
With twenty pillows for her head.
The frog said,
"It would be a treat
If I could sleep
right at your feet."

The princess was not too impressed
With this arrangement for her guest.

"Oh, no," she said,
"you'll take the floor.
I can't be near you anymore.
I'll have no slime stain left as proof
A frog has slept beneath my roof."

The king gave her an angry look.
He shouted so the stone walls shook.

"What you have promised, you must do!
Can't you see frogs have feelings too?
Your frog friend will sleep on that bed,
Or you'll be dungeon-bound instead."

The princess saw, to her dismay,
She had no choice but to obey.
She picked the frog up with regret
And set him on her coverlet.

The king said,
"Not another peep!
Now get in bed and go to sleep."

The princess was consumed by fear.
She didn't want the frog so near.
So as her father left the room,
She sought escape
from certain doom.

She said,
"Frog, your request does seem
To me to be a bit extreme.
My foolish pledge was, I'm afraid,
A promise I should not have made.
But luckily, it's not too late;
I'm sure we can negotiate.
If you stay up there, warm and snug,
Then I'll sleep here, upon the rug."

The frog replied, "I will agree
If you do one small thing for me:
Before you douse the candlelight,
Will you give me a kiss goodnight?"

The princess flinched, and with a shriek,
She shouted, "No, you slimy freak!"

And in that moment,
she could see
The frog have an epiphany.

He said,
"Why's that so hard to do?
I don't know what is wrong with you,
Or why I ever asked to be
Your friend until eternity."

And then the frog began to cry.
She didn't know how to reply.

She suddenly felt very bad.
At last she saw frogs could feel sad.
"I'm sorry," she said finally.
"That wasn't very nice of me.

"I will try harder to be kind,
And you can stay here, I don't mind.
But friendship, you must understand,
Cannot be given on command."

The frog was silent for a while,
And then said, with a rueful smile,
"Well, since you can't
be friends with me,
'Tis better we part company.
So princess, listen closely now:
I will release you from your vow
If you give me a kiss goodbye.
I need that kiss.
Please don't ask why."

The princess frowned. She said, "I'd give
My crown for an alternative."
          "That's not enough," she heard him scoff.
              "A kiss, or else our deal is off."

The princess looked at him askance.
The frog said, "You have one last chance.
Just kiss me once, and princess, then
I'll never bother you again."

A kiss was a high price to pay.
She hoped he'd really go away.
"All right," the princess sighed, "I'll try,
Although I'm feeling very shy."

The frog hopped to the floor below.
The princess blushed from head to toe.
She closed her eyes, tried not to peek,
And brushed her lips against his cheek.

His skin was wet and cold and rough.
She pulled away; she'd had enough.
And then the strangest thing occurred.
At first she thought her vision blurred.

The frog was gone!
He had been since
Transformed into
a handsome prince.
The princess blinked.
She stumbled back.
She thought
she'd had a heart attack.

And then
she figured something out.
"Is that what this was all about?
You tricked me into kissing you!"
The princess cried.

The prince said, "True.
A witch transformed my skin and bone,
And then she seized my father's throne.
The curse could only be undone
By you, the chosen of the Sun.
I had one chance to be set free:
You had to kiss me willingly."

The princess said, "I wish I'd known.
I wouldn't have felt so alone."

The prince laughed. "I regret to say
That magic doesn't work that way,
For much is hidden from our view.
The spell would not break if you knew."

The king learned of the frog-prince guise
And said, "That's not a big surprise.
I thought you seemed too shrewd, my son,
To be a mere amphibian."

"I'm so glad that I broke the spell,"
The princess said. "Now all is well.
Prince, please do let me make amends.
The truth is, I've not many friends."

The prince consented, and he stayed,
And every single day they played.
She learned to share her toys with him.
He even taught her how to swim.

And as a happy consequence,
They fell in love a few years hence.
Upon their wedding day the Sun
Shone warmly down on everyone.

The frog prince and his princess bride
Were celebrated far and wide.
And people still tell, to this day,
Of that cold realm so far away,

The cunning youth, and selfish lass,
And how their union came to pass,
And how—save for that golden ball—
They never would have met at all.

How to Read This Book Aloud

The Golden Ball is written in a poetic form called iambic tetrameter. Each set of eight syllables is divided into four two-syllable increments called iambic "feet." (In general, each printed line is also eight syllables long—but due to some creative typesetting, not always.)

In each iambic foot, the first syllable is weaker, or unstressed ("da"), and the second is stronger, or stressed ("DUM"). The pattern of stresses for reading a line of the poem aloud can be represented by the sequence:

da **DUM** da **DUM** da **DUM** da **DUM**

The text also rhymes regularly, in pairs of lines called couplets. The first stanza of **The Golden Ball** should be stressed like this:

An **IN**-fant **PRIN**-cess **ONCE** was **BORN**
U-**PON** an **EAR**-ly **WIN**-ter **MORN**
So **LONG** a-**GO** and **FAR** a-**WAY**
Her **NAME** is **LOST** to **US** to-**DAY**.

Continue to use this rhythmic pattern throughout the book. To hear **The Golden Ball** read aloud from beginning to end, please visit **www.katelynsinclair.com**.

CPSIA information can be obtained
at www.ICGtesting.com
Printed in the USA
259235LV00001B